Cover: *Detail from* Battle of Pea Ridge, Arkansas, *c. 1889, by Kurz & Allison*

CMH Pub 75-3

THE CIVIL WAR IN THE TRANS-MISSISSIPPI THEATER

1861–1865

by
Jeffery S. Prushankin

Reprinted by St. John's Press LLC
Alexandria, Va. 22301
ISBN 978-1944961039
2016
Center of Military History United
States Army Washington, D.C.,
2015

INTRODUCTION

Although over one hundred fifty years have passed since the start of the American Civil War, that titanic conflict continues to matter. The forces unleashed by that war were immensely destructive because of the significant issues involved: the existence of the Union, the end of slavery, and the very future of the nation. The war remains our most contentious, and our bloodiest, with over six hundred thousand killed in the course of the four-year struggle.

Most civil wars do not spring up overnight, and the American Civil War was no exception. The seeds of the conflict were sown in the earliest days of the republic's founding, primarily over the existence of slavery and the slave trade. Although no conflict can begin without the conscious decisions of those engaged in the debates at that moment, in the end, there was simply no way to paper over the division of the country into two camps: one that was dominated by slavery and the other that sought first to limit its spread and then to abolish it. Our nation was indeed "half slave and half free," and that could not stand.

Regardless of the factors tearing the nation asunder, the soldiers on each side of the struggle went to war for personal reasons: looking for adventure, being caught up in the passions and emotions of their peers, believing in the Union, favoring states' rights, or even justifying the simple schoolyard dynamic of being convinced that they were "worth" three of the soldiers on the other side. Nor can we overlook the factor that some went to war to prove their manhood. This has been, and continues to be, a key dynamic in understanding combat and the profession of arms. Soldiers join for many reasons but often stay in the fight because of their comrades and because they do not want to seem like cowards. Sometimes issues of national impact shrink to nothing in the intensely personal world of cannon shell and minié ball.

Whatever the reasons, the struggle was long and costly and only culminated with the conquest of the rebellious Confederacy, the preservation of the Union, and the end of slavery. These campaign pamphlets on the American Civil War, prepared in commemoration of our national sacrifices, seek to remember that war and honor those in the United States Army who died to preserve the Union and free the slaves as well as to tell the story of those American soldiers who fought for the Confederacy despite the inherently flawed nature of their cause. The Civil War was our greatest struggle and continues to deserve our deep study and contemplation.

RICHARD W. STEWART, PH.D.
Chief of Military History

THE CIVIL WAR IN THE
TRANS-MISSISSIPPI THEATER
1861–1865

Strategic Setting

Often neglected in history books, the Trans-Mississippi West played an important role in the Civil War. Although the battles fought in this region were relatively small compared with those fought elsewhere, the struggle to control the Trans-Mississippi had far-reaching consequences for both sides (*Map 1*).

For the Union, the theater presented several major objectives. At the outset of the war, President Abraham Lincoln's first concern in the region west of the Mississippi River was securing the state of Missouri and its principal city, St. Louis. Until the military accomplished this objective, it would be difficult to achieve the broader strategic goal of severing the Confederacy in two by gaining control of the Mississippi. Second, the United States hoped to pacify western Louisiana and establish a presence in Texas. While all of the Trans-Mississippi states had the potential to provide the Confederacy with resources, Texas gave the Confederacy its only common border with a foreign country. Since France had invaded Mexico in December 1861 over issues related to unpaid debts, U.S. officials feared that the Confederacy might be able to acquire European goods in exchange for cotton via Mexico,

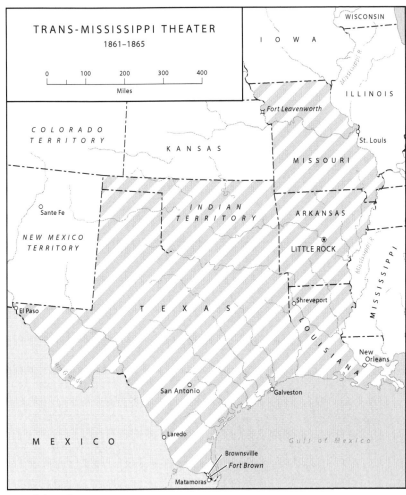

MAP 1

thereby defeating the government's planned blockade of Southern ports. If France recognized the Confederacy as an independent nation, its presence on the Texas border could prove even more dangerous. Finally, the Lincoln administration wanted to ensure that the Federal government maintained control of the Far West, to include the gold deposits in Colorado and California.

For the Confederacy, the Trans-Mississippi was an important source of agricultural commodities, including cotton, sugar, and rice. The southwestern part of the region contained

8

nearly one million horses, 800,000 oxen, over 300,000 mules, and millions of cattle. The area was likewise a source of manpower. During the course of the war Texas furnished 58,000 men for Confederate armies, Louisiana provided 53,000, and Arkansas sent 45,000. Missouri and Indian Territory did not secede from the Union, but nonetheless sent 40,000 and 5,000 men, respectively, into rebel service. Although most of these Trans-Mississippians served in eastern armies, enough soldiers remained west of the river to protect the Confederate political and economic infrastructure in the theater.

The region's vast distances and primitive transportation and communication networks posed challenges for both sides during the war. Early in 1862, the Confederate War Department created a Trans-Mississippi District and later that year elevated the Trans-Mississippi to department status. The U.S. Army never created a single entity to command its forces west of the Mississippi. Rather, it organized several geographically based military departments. During the conflict the War Department continually adjusted existing designations and often combined two or more departments to create military divisions. Individual field armies functioned within each department. In the Trans-Mississippi the principle Federal armies included the Army of the Southwest, the Army of the Frontier, and the Army of the Gulf. State and local authorities often complicated command relationships, particularly for the South, so that military forces did not always act in concert with one another. During the course of the war, some 200,000 Union soldiers would serve in the Trans-Mississippi Theater.

Operations

WAR IN THE DESERT

The most remote area of operations during the American Civil War was that in the far western territories of New Mexico and Arizona. The American Southwest was a sparsely inhabited land of divided loyalties. In New Mexico, the population around Santa Fe was predominately neutral, while settlers farther south called themselves Arizonians and harbored pro-Confederate sentiments. In 1861, Confederate sympathizers decreed Arizona a territory. To secure that claim, and with hopes of conquering New Mexico, Colorado, Utah, and perhaps even California, rebel Brig. Gen. Henry H. Sibley organized a force of 3,700 men that he called the

Army of New Mexico. In February 1862 he marched north along the Rio Grande from El Paso, Texas, toward Fort Craig, south of Albuquerque, New Mexico. At this post there were 1,250 U.S. Army regulars and over 1,000 recently raised New Mexico volunteers and militia. After having failed to draw the Federal commander, Col. Edward R. S. Canby, out of his works, Sibley decided to bypass the fort through the high bluffs to the east. Canby responded by intercepting the rebels at Valverde Ford on the Rio Grande on 20 February. The next day, the Federals met Sibley's advance, but suffered a defeat after a Confederate charge captured their artillery (*Map 2*).

Colonel Canby, pictured as a general
(Library of Congress)

Canby fell back into the fort and refused to surrender, compelling Sibley to leave behind a detachment to watch the post while he proceeded northward to Santa Fe through inhospitable country. As Sibley's force grew weaker because of the harsh conditions, the Federals to his front grew stronger. Unionists from Colorado rushed to support Federal forces in New Mexico, and on 26 March, a portion of the Confederate advance clashed with the Colorado volunteers at Apache Canyon near Glorieta Pass, about twenty-five miles east of Santa Fe. Both sides concentrated their forces, and on 28 March, skirmishing near Pigeon's Ranch, just east of Glorieta Pass, erupted into a pitched battle. Although Sibley's forces drove the Federals from the field, Maj. John M. Chivington, from Colorado, attacked the Confederate rear and destroyed the rebels' supply wagons. Chivington's feat rendered Sibley's tactical victory meaningless and forced the Confederates to abandon the campaign. Canby pursued Sibley's defeated army for several days but did not attempt to bring it to battle. Still, the Confederates, lacking supplies, endured a punishing retreat, first to El Paso, and then on to San Antonio, Texas.

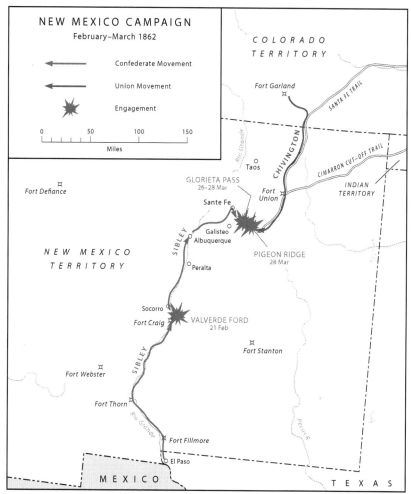

MAP 2

The Confederate repulse brought an end to significant fighting in the far western territories.

THE BATTLE FOR MISSOURI AND ARKANSAS

The only Trans-Mississippi slave state remaining in the Union, Missouri, was the linchpin for the U.S. government's ability to use military force on the Mississippi River and the lands beyond. Control of St. Louis would allow the U.S. military to establish lines of communications along the Mississippi River and along the road network that connected the city to points to the north, west, and south. Missouri was a divided state, however, and many citizens held strong pro-Confederate sympathies. The United States strengthened its military presence in St. Louis by reinforcing Capt. Nathaniel Lyon and his 2d United States Infantry stationed there. The pro-Confederate state militia camped just outside of town, and Lyon feared it would attempt to seize the St. Louis arsenal. On 10 May, in a preemptive strike, he arrested 600 militia members. As he marched the prisoners through town, rioting broke out, and Lyon's troops killed over two dozen civilians. Tensions continued to rise as the War Department promoted Lyon to brigadier general and authorized some 10,000 troops to serve under him in Missouri. Lyon's next move was against pro-Confederate politicians at the state capital in Jefferson City. In June, his force drove the nascent Confederates to the southwest corner of the state.

In the summer of 1861, the United States could not risk leaving the situation in Missouri unresolved. A Confederate resurgence would threaten not only St. Louis, but also possibly Kansas and Illinois. Fearing that Confederates in northwest Arkansas would join Brig. Gen. Sterling Price's secessionist Missouri State Guard in the southwest portion of Missouri in late July, General Lyon gathered 5,400 troops into what he called the Army of the West and marched into south-western Missouri. (*See Map 3.*) Soon after he arrived at Springfield, Missouri, Lyon discovered that Brig. Gen. Ben McCulloch's Western Army, a Confederate force that included Price's Missouri State Guard among its 11,000 effectives, was fifty miles to the southeast at Cassville. The Confederates advanced toward Springfield and Lyon planned to attack isolated elements of the rebel column. After a skirmish on 2 August at Dug Spring, he reconsidered and fell back ahead of McCulloch's superior force.

General Lyon, shown as captain
(Library of Congress)

General Price
(Library of Congress)

General McCulloch
(Library of Congress)

McCulloch hoped to drive Lyon from southwest Missouri as a means of protecting northwest Arkansas and the Indian Territory, while Price saw the capture of Springfield as the first step in regaining control of his home state. On 9 August, bad weather delayed the Confederate advance, and when McCulloch paused along Wilson's Creek, twelve miles south of Springfield, Lyon seized the initiative.

Lyon accepted a plan offered by Col. Franz Sigel to divide his army and launch simultaneous surprise attacks against the enemy flanks. At dawn on 10 August, the Federals hit the unsuspecting Confederates. Striking from the north, Lyon and his 4,200 men caught the rebels off guard. From the south, Sigel and his column of 1,200 men likewise enjoyed initial success, but McCulloch rallied the Confederates and Sigel soon withdrew in disorder, leaving behind most of his artillery. This allowed the Confederates to take the offensive. Unaware of Sigel's retreat, Lyon put up a ferocious defensive fight along a ridge known later as Bloody Hill. Price's Missourians also fought tenaciously, and the battle turned in favor of the Confederates. During the fighting, Lyon was killed, the first U.S. Army general officer to die in combat during the Civil War. Union command devolved to Maj. Samuel D. Sturgis, who continued to hold the position at Bloody Hill until he learned of Sigel's retreat. With ammunition

*Colonel Sigel, shown as
major general
(Library of Congress)*

*Major Sturgis, shown as
brigadier general
(Library of Congress)*

running low, Sturgis ordered a withdrawal to Springfield and by 1200, the Federals were gone.

The Battle of Wilson's Creek left the Federals with 1,317 casualties, including 258 killed and 873 wounded. The Confederates, who called the battle Oak Hill, suffered similar losses, with 1,222 casualties, including 277 dead and 945 wounded. As the first major battle in the Trans-Mississippi, Wilson's Creek set into motion events that shaped the prosecution of the war in the West.

The Confederate victory at Wilson's Creek rendered the Federal hold on Springfield untenable. Sigel assumed command of the Army of the West and ordered a retreat to Rolla in central Missouri. During the retreat, Union officers and enlisted men alike criticized Sigel's performance at Wilson's Creek, and he relinquished command to Major Sturgis. From Rolla, a rail line took the troops to St. Louis where Maj. Gen. John C. Frémont, commander of the United States Western Department, reassigned the units and officers to other commands.

Frémont was an antebellum adventurer, abolitionist, and the Republican Party presidential nominee in 1856. In 1861, it was political influence, rather than military prowess, that earned him a generalship in the Union Army. Frémont had taken command of the department in July, and since his arrival in Missouri, he had

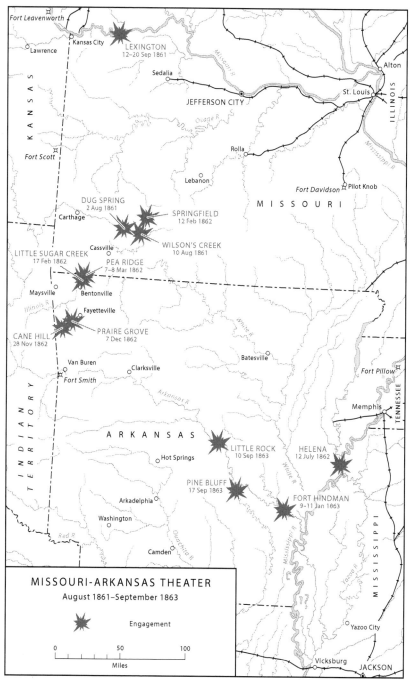

Fort Leavenworth
Kansas City
Lawrence
LEXINGTON
12–20 Sep 1861
Sedalia
JEFFERSON CITY
St. Louis
Alton
ILLINOIS
Missouri R.

K A N S A S
Osage R.
Rolla
Fort Scott
Lebanon
Fort Davidson Pilot Knob
M I S S O U R I
DUG SPRING
2 Aug 1861
Carthage
SPRINGFIELD
12 Feb 1862
Cassville
WILSON'S CREEK
10 Aug 1861
LITTLE SUGAR CREEK
17 Feb 1862
Maysville
PEA RIDGE
7–8 Mar 1862
Bentonville
Illinois R.
Fayetteville
White R.
Batesville
CANE HILL
28 Nov 1862
PRAIRE GROVE
7 Dec 1862
Fort Pillow
Van Buren
Clarksville
Fort Smith
Arkansas R.
Memphis
TENNESSEE
I N D I A N   T E R R I T O R Y
A R K A N S A S
LITTLE ROCK
10 Sep 1863
HELENA
12 July 1862
Hot Springs
PINE BLUFF
17 Sep 1863
Arkadelphia
FORT HINDMAN
9–11 Jan 1863
White R.
Washington
Red R.
M I S S I S S I P P I
Camden
Ouachita R.
Mississippi R.
Yazoo R.

MISSOURI-ARKANSAS THEATER
August 1861–September 1863

Engagement

0   50   100
Miles

Yazoo City
Vicksburg
JACKSON

MAP 3

busied himself with organizing his forces. He did not have time to focus on internal dissent, particularly on the heels of Wilson's Creek. Moreover, Price was on the move, and the Confederates had retaken Springfield.

Like the Federals, Confederate commanders bickered among themselves. General Price, who held his commission from the state of Missouri, insisted on advancing north to Lexington, a city on the Missouri River, to recruit volunteers for the State Guard. General McCulloch, who held a commission from the Confederate government, refused to sanction the mission and insisted that he did not have authorization to conduct offensive operations in Missouri. He considered the earlier movement toward Springfield a defensive measure, designed to help him achieve his primary mission of securing Arkansas and the Indian Territory. Price's plan was more offensive in nature. Moreover, McCulloch insisted that the Confederates lacked the means and manpower to hold positions around Lexington. The disagreement left Price embittered, and as he marched his Missourians to Lexington, McCulloch marched the Western Army to Arkansas.

General Frémont
(Library of Congress)

On 12 September, Price reached Lexington, and as recruits flocked to his command, the State Guard increased to nearly 18,000 men. For nine days, Price's force besieged the town and pinned down the small Union garrison of 3,800 Federals under Col. James A. Mulligan. The town fell on 20 September when a majority of Colonel Mulligan's subordinate officers voted to surrender.

General Frémont's failure to reinforce the garrison at Lexington left him open to criticism. He responded quickly and pushed 30,000 troops west from St. Louis to confront the Missouri State Guard. Price realized that his position was untenable and fell back toward the Arkansas line ahead of Frémont's advance. In late October, the Federals marched into Springfield.

Frémont provoked controversy with a declaration of martial law, alienating many civilians and politicians. His decision to confiscate the property of Confederate sympathizers, including slaves, exceeded his authority as department commander. On 2 November, President Lincoln relieved him and appointed Maj. Gen. David Hunter to command. Hunter withdrew the army to the Sedalia-Rolla line and scattered his forces across the central and eastern portions of the state. Meanwhile, Price's State Guard secured positions around Springfield.

On 19 November, the War Department transferred General Hunter to command the Department of Kansas and appointed Maj. Gen. Henry W. Halleck in his place. Nicknamed "Old Brains," Halleck often took a theoretical approach to war and applied his considerable intellectual prowess to solving military problems. In Missouri, he recognized the need to secure St. Louis as the base of operations for a spring campaign to control the Mississippi River. Accordingly, he designed a campaign to "drive Price from the state," thereby ridding Missouri of the Confederate threat and releasing Union troops for operations to secure the Mississippi.

On 25 December, Halleck appointed Brig. Gen. Samuel R. Curtis to command the Military District of Southwest Missouri and instructed him to lead the 12,000-man Army of the Southwest against Price. In mid-January 1862, Curtis organized his forces at Lebanon, some fifty miles southwest of his supply base at Rolla and sixty miles northeast of Springfield, his immediate objective. Curtis appointed General Sigel second-in-command and gave him control of a corps of two small divisions: the 1st Division under Col. Peter J. Osterhaus, a Prussian, and the 2d Division under Brig. Gen. Alexander S. Asboth, a Hungarian. A large number of German immigrants from St. Louis made up these divisions, and Curtis took Sigel's German ethnicity into consideration. Nevertheless, relations between Curtis and Sigel remained strained for the duration of the campaign. The rest of the army consisted of the 3d Division under Col. Jefferson C. Davis, a regular Army veteran from Indiana, and the 4th Division, led by Col. Eugene A. Carr.

Curtis' advance units approached Springfield on 12 February and took the Confederates by surprise. Price had not anticipated a winter offensive by the Federals and had failed to prepare adequate fortifications. He had 8,000 men at Springfield, but with General

General Curtis
(Library of Congress)

McCulloch's command in Northwest Arkansas, the Confederates could not effect a concentration in time. Price ordered an expeditious retreat down the Telegraph Road toward the state line. Curtis paused in Springfield long enough to secure the town and then pursued Price. For Curtis and Halleck, possession of Springfield itself meant little without putting an end to the Confederate presence in Missouri, and that meant the destruction of Price's army.

With Price in flight, Curtis had to take decisive action to catch the Confederates before they escaped Missouri. He disregarded Halleck's admonition to keep his forces together and, at Sigel's behest, divided the army. Curtis pushed the 3d and 4th Divisions down the Telegraph Road while Sigel's command moved along a parallel series of roads to the west in an attempt to get in front of Price. Snow, ice, and freezing conditions slowed the movement of both columns. A Missouri Confederate noted that "snow was all over us, and our clothes frozen to our bodies." Curtis failed to prevent Price's escape, and on 16 February, the Confederates crossed into Arkansas. Rather than stop at the state line, however, Curtis continued the pursuit.

Just inside Arkansas, the Federals encountered stiff resistance near Little Sugar Creek. Unbeknownst to Curtis, elements of McCulloch's command under Col. Louis Hebert had come up to support Price. Curtis halted pursuit and took stock of his situation. Already 250 miles from the supply depot at Rolla he did not want to extend his lines of communications deeper into enemy territory, particularly if, as he suspected, the Confederates were in strong force. Halleck instructed Curtis to secure his position and await support. Meanwhile, the Confederates evacuated Fayetteville, Arkansas, and concentrated their forces twenty-five miles to the south in the Boston Mountains.

The Confederates had a new commander, Maj. Gen. Earl Van Dorn, an impetuous U.S. Military Academy graduate from Mississippi. Recent squabbles between generals Price and McCulloch concerning troop dispositions and command responsibilities had prompted Confederate President Jefferson Davis to designate the Trans-Mississippi as a separate military district and to appoint an overall commander. Van Dorn arrived in late January and consolidated the forces of McCulloch, Price, some Texas cavalry units, and a brigade of American Indians under Brig. Gen. Albert Pike, to create a new army, the 16,000-man Army of the West. Van Dorn planned a spring campaign to capture St. Louis. The Federals, however, had seized the initiative and by the end of February, Curtis held the road network in northwest Arkansas as well as good defensive ground behind Little Sugar Creek along a broad plateau known as Pea Ridge.

General Van Dorn
(Library of Congress)

Van Dorn devised a plan to regain the strategic initiative by destroying the Union Army of the Southwest. He would first strike Sigel's force at Bentonville, Arkansas, then turn east to fall on Curtis. Once Van Dorn disposed of the Federals in northwest Arkansas, he would have a clear road to Springfield and St. Louis. Van Dorn's plan to concentrate superior force against divided elements of the enemy was sound. In addition, the Confederates had the element of surprise working in their favor. However, bad weather, a lack of supplies, and poor staff work undermined Confederate efforts.

Van Dorn's army advanced from the Boston Mountains on 4 March, but the next day Unionists in northwest Arkansas alerted Curtis to the rebel movements. On 6 March Curtis concentrated his troops at a fortified position astride the Telegraph Road, north of Little Sugar Creek. When General Van Dorn neared Bentonville, he realized that Sigel had fled and that Curtis had concentrated his army in a defensive position to the east. That night at a council-of-war, General McCulloch identified a road called the Bentonville Detour that ran around Curtis' right and led to the Telegraph Road near Cross Timber Hollow, five miles to the rear of the Union position. McCulloch suggested a flanking movement with part of the rebel army to force Curtis out of his entrenchments and compel his retreat to Missouri. Van Dorn, however, envisioned a grand flanking maneuver with his entire command to envelop the enemy position completely and force Curtis to surrender. Van Dorn ordered the Confederates to begin the operation at once, although McCulloch and Price protested that the men were exhausted and hungry. Nevertheless, by 2400, the Confederates were on the march.

Meanwhile, the Federals did not stand by idly and await attack. On the afternoon of 6 March, Curtis created defensive positions that commanded clear fields of fire to his front and flanks. He also secured avenues of approach on all sides. At the suggestion of Col. Grenville M. Dodge, he ordered trees felled across the Bentonville Detour to slow any Confederate attempt at a flanking maneuver.

By dawn, only General Price's command had reached the Telegraph Road in the rear of Curtis' line, while McCulloch's men remained strung out along the Bentonville Detour. Realizing that McCulloch could not reach the staging ground at Cross Timber Hollow until midafternoon, Van Dorn divided the army. He ordered Price to move south along the Telegraph Road to the Elkhorn Tavern. Meanwhile, McCulloch would march two and a half miles along the Ford Road, a farm lane that ran east below the southern face of a sprawling hill known as Big Mountain. The path would carry McCulloch to the Telegraph Road just below Elkhorn Tavern and two miles above Curtis at Little Sugar Creek. At that point, McCulloch and Price would reunite to confront the Federals.

On the morning of 7 March, Curtis expected the main Confederate attack to come from the south against his front. He realized, however, that a contingent of Confederates had indeed turned his right. Therefore, he ordered Colonel Osterhaus, whose division held the Union right, to conduct a reconnaissance in force, advancing north from Little Sugar Creek toward Leetown and the Bentonville Detour. (*See Map 4.*)

Moving north along the Leetown Road, Osterhaus spotted several thousand Confederates marching directly across his front headed east on the Ford Road toward the Telegraph Road. He realized that this was not a diversionary force but General McCulloch's entire command, over 8,000 strong. "I could not hesitate in my course of action" Osterhaus reported, "the safety of our position was dependent upon the securing of our right flank and the keeping back of the enemy until I was re-enforced." He deployed several companies of his cavalry under Col. Cyrus Bussey into line of battle and, with his artillery, opened on the Confederates. The attack took the latter by surprise, but McCulloch deployed 3,000 cavalrymen under Brig. Gen. James M. McIntosh, whose charge routed the outmanned Federals. Osterhaus brought up reinforcements, formed a line at Oberson's Field, and directed his artillery to fire over the trees at the Confederates occupying Foster's farm.

Despite his initial repulse, Osterhaus had accomplished his immediate objective of delaying the Confederate attempt to concentrate at Elkhorn Tavern. Rather than risk leaving a Federal force in his rear, McCulloch decided to stay and fight. Before ordering his attack to commence, however, he was killed reconnoitering the Federal lines. Command devolved to General

Battle of Pea Ridge, Ark.
(Library of Congress)

McIntosh, who sent orders to launch the attack. McIntosh chose to lead from the front, and in the course of the attack he too fell. The loss of two commanding officers in fewer than two hours stunned the division. Leaderless, and without a clear understanding of the objectives, Confederate field officers pulled their troops back.

Confederate command fell on Colonel Hebert, whose Arkansas brigade held the flank east of the Leetown Road. Hebert did not know what had happened to the rebels across the road, and poor communications left him unaware of his new status as division commander. Upon hearing the fire to the west, Hebert sent his brigade forward. The thick woods disrupted the brigade's alignment and they soon came under fire from Union artillery. The Federals held back the Confederates for nearly forty-five minutes until Hebert's superior numbers began to turn the fight in his favor. When the Confederates broke through the battery, Indiana troops under Col. Thomas Patterson arrived and the Federals pitched into the rebel's left flank as other regiments opened on the enemy right. Under fire from three sides, the unsupported Confederates fell back in disorder as the Federals took numerous prisoners, including Colonel Hebert. Colonel Osterhaus thus had achieved

East front of the Elkhorn Tavern, Pea Ridge, c.1886
(Library of Congress)

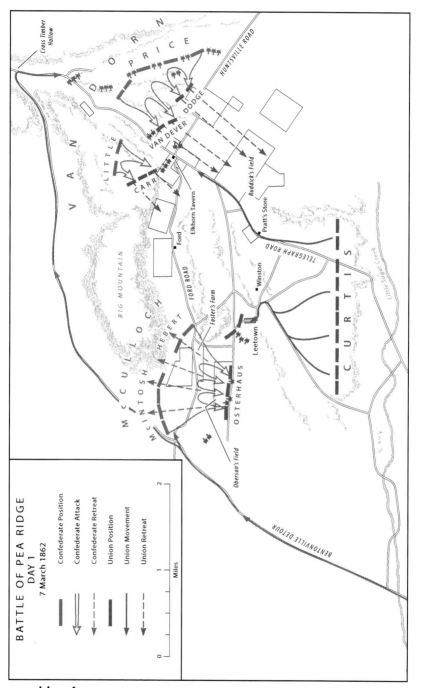

BATTLE OF PEA RIDGE
DAY 1
7 March 1862

Confederate Position
Confederate Attack
Confederate Retreat
Union Position
Union Movement
Union Retreat

Miles
0   1   2

MAP 4

two objectives—he had secured the right flank of the Union army by uncovering the Confederate turning movement and he had prevented the rebels from concentrating both wings of General Van Dorn's army in Curtis' rear.

As the fighting unfolded at Leetown, General Curtis received word of a Southern force massing several miles to his rear along the Telegraph Road in Cross Timber Hollow. Curtis discerned the Confederate strategy and took steps to address the threat to his rear. He ordered Colonel Carr, commander of the 4th Division, to send Colonel Dodge's brigade north on the Telegraph Road to the Elkhorn Tavern, a way station that stood at the southern edge of Cross Timber Hollow on the Pea Ridge plateau. Dodge posted his men along the high ground overlooking the approach to Pea Ridge. His left rested between the tavern and a rise known as Big Mountain while his right extended east along the Huntsville Road. Carr had the bulk of the Union army to his rear with an unknown Confederate force to his front. Despite the favorable ground, Carr recognized the need for more men to secure the position, and Curtis instructed him to bring up the rest of his division, a brigade under Col. William Vandever. Around 1200, as Vandever deployed his infantry, Carr ordered a battery to fire on suspected Confederate positions about one-half mile away. Rebel guns promptly returned the fire.

The sudden firing took both the Federals and Confederates by surprise. Carr did not expect to discover half of the Confederate army deployed into line of battle north of his front, while Price and Van Dorn did not anticipate meeting the Federals until they neared Little Sugar Creek. For over two hours firing filled the hollows with dense smoke. Price was shot in the arm but remained in command of his division. Although the Confederates outnumbered Carr's force by over two-to-one, the Federals held the high ground, and Van Dorn did not press the advantage. Unaware of the troubles along Ford Road, he undoubtedly hoped McCulloch would arrive to unhinge the Federal left at Elkhorn Tavern. Only after learning of the battle at Leetown did Van Dorn shift to the tactical offensive. He instructed Price to ascend Pea Ridge and roll up the Union right flank on the Huntsville Road while Col. Lewis Henry Little's Missouri brigade attacked the Federal left at Elkhorn Tavern. If successful, the Confederates would crush the Federals in a vise.

The assault got underway late in the afternoon. On the Union right, Colonel Dodge anticipated the Confederates and ordered his brigade to refuse its thin line. Dodge's infantry held a strong position along a belt of woods bordering the Clemons Field, but with only two guns, he could do little to answer Price's artillery. After enduring nearly twenty minutes of shot and shell, Dodge's men braced for Confederate infantry. General Price committed his troops piecemeal, and the Federals repelled the attack. Price repeated the pattern of artillery followed by infantry but again failed to utilize his numerical strength, and the Confederates fell back a second time. Finally, Price used the woods to conceal the movement of a portion of his command while another contingent struck Dodge's brigade head on. The Federals gave ground grudgingly and retreated toward the Telegraph Road.

Things were no better for Colonel Vandever's brigade on the Union left as the Confederates seized Elkhorn Tavern. Colonel Carr ordered a retreat and his division withdrew down the Telegraph Road for nearly one-half mile before officers directed them to re-form along the woods south of Ruddick's cornfield. Vandever's brigade held a position with their left on the Telegraph Road and Dodge's brigade to their right.

The Confederate pursuit was ragged, and at dusk elements of Price's division finally emerged from the woods north of Ruddick's field. They found the Federals in line of battle supported by thirteen guns. Flush from the rout at Elkhorn Tavern and undeterred by the strong Union position, the rebels advanced across the field. Many of Price's Missourians wore newly issued, undyed, wool uniforms that stood out as bright white against the darkness, and Union musketry cut them down by the score. Again, the Confederates failed to take advantage of superior numbers and fell back into the woods. During the fighting General Curtis arrived on the field and, sensing a chance to regain ground around Elkhorn Tavern, personally led some 500 reinforcements up the Telegraph Road. He ordered Dodge to take the 4th Iowa Infantry and join the sortie but as the troops pushed forward, Confederate artillery opened on them, and the Federals fell back.

In the day's fighting around Elkhorn Tavern, the Confederates had squandered numerous opportunities. Van Dorn's failure to immediately seize the tactical initiative in Cross Timber Hollow gave Curtis time to shift Carr from Little Sugar Creek to Elkhorn Tavern and delay the Confederate advance. Once the Confederates launched an all out attack, Carr made good use of the terrain and, rather than yield the ground to superior numbers, forced Van Dorn to claw his way up from Cross Timber Hollow to Pea Ridge. By the time the fighting on the Huntsville Road and at Elkhorn Tavern became general, Curtis knew that he had been turned and took steps to reorient his front 180 degrees from Little Sugar Creek to face the Confederate threat from the north. Nevertheless, the Confederates could have pushed the Federals at Ruddick's Field, but they again failed to bring superior numbers to bear. Personal gallantry notwithstanding, Curtis displayed strong, if not deliberate leadership and, despite the bold vision of his Southern counterpart, out-generaled Van Dorn.

Throughout the night of 7 March, the Federals completed their redeployment of the face of their front from south to north and sent the army's supply trains to safety south of Little Sugar Creek. General Curtis also recalled Colonel Davis' division from Leetown to extend Carr's left across the Telegraph Road south of Ruddick's Field. General Van Dorn attempted to consolidate his forces along the Telegraph Road below Elkhorn Tavern, but by dawn, nearly half of the troops from Leetown had not arrived. He positioned McCulloch's men, now under General Pike, astride the Telegraph Road but divided General Price's division, placing the Missouri State Guard on the eastern flank and the 1st and 2d Missouri brigades to the west. Moreover, the wooded heights known as Big Mountain hemmed in the Confederate right and constrained infantry movements. Although Big Mountain was a poor place for infantry, it provided a strong artillery platform. Yet, Van Dorn either failed to recognize this or simply did not foresee the need to turn this terrain to his advantage. Further complicating the situation for Van Dorn, Confederate trains made a wrong turn on the Bentonville Detour and had moved away from the Telegraph Road. Consequently, at dawn on 8 March, the Confederate ranks were thin and poorly aligned, as well as short of food, medicine, and munitions.

The Federals expected Van Dorn to initiate battle at dawn, but when a Confederate advance failed to materialize, Colonel Davis unleashed his artillery to probe the enemy position north of Ruddick's Field (*Map 5*). The Confederates returned a concentrated artillery barrage toward Davis' position, and the Federal left or western flank began to bend back. The artillery duel had uncovered the Confederate position, and Curtis sensed an opportunity to take the tactical initiative. He directed General Sigel to hurry his divisions from Little Sugar Creek and form on the left of Davis'

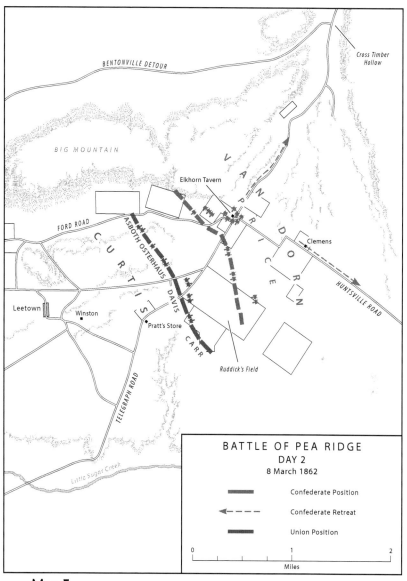

Cross Timber
Hollow

BENTONVILLE DETOUR

BIG MOUNTAIN

V
A
N

Elkhorn Tavern

D
O
R
N

FORD ROAD

C
U
R
T
I
S

ASBOTH OSTERHAUS

DAVIS

Clemens

HUNTSVILLE ROAD

Leetown

Winston

Pratt's Store

C
A
R
R

Ruddick's Field

TELEGRAPH ROAD

Little Sugar Creek

BATTLE OF PEA RIDGE
DAY 2
8 March 1862

Confederate Position

Confederate Retreat

Union Position

0   1   2

Miles

MAP 5

division. Sigel moved quickly and placed Osterhaus' division between Davis' left and a rise of ground, later called Welfey's Knoll, while General Asboth aligned his command at a slight angle left of Osterhaus' men. The Union line soon stretched nearly one mile and extended past the Confederate flanks. Moreover, the Union had more guns and a strong artillery platform. Around 0800, with deployments completed, Curtis ordered the artillery to open ahead of the infantry advance.

After a two-hour artillery battle Van Dorn realized the situation was hopeless and ordered a retreat eastward on the Huntsville Road before directing his army to march south to Van Buren, some one hundred miles distant. Troops already in line of battle would fight a rear guard action to protect the withdrawal and then join the retreat. About 1030, 10,000 Federal troops advanced against rebels at the Elkhorn Tavern. In the face of the onslaught, the Confederate line collapsed, precipitating a confused and disorderly rebel retreat. The confusion actually worked to the rebels' advantage. The Federals did not know in which direction Van Dorn's main force had fled, and so Curtis did not launch a full-scale pursuit.

The battle was costly to both sides. Of the 10,250 engaged, the Federals suffered 1,384 casualties, a rate of 14 percent. Casualties were worse for the Confederates as Van Dorn lost 2,000 of the 12,500 men engaged, a 16 percent casualty rate. Two weeks later, when most of the Confederates reached Van Buren, the Army of the West was a shell of its former self with limited combat capabilities and little esprit de corps. For the Confederates, the campaign to regain Missouri had been a disaster. For the Federals, however, the Pea Ridge Campaign had accomplished its dual objectives of destroying Price's army and saving Missouri for the Union, at least for the time being.

The Union Army of the Southwest moved east to secure the Missouri border while Van Dorn's army crossed the Mississippi, intending to join Confederate forces at Corinth for operations against Maj. Gen. Ulysses S. Grant in Tennessee. Van Dorn's removal left the Confederates in the Trans-Mississippi without an organized military force to contest Union troop movements. With the Confederate Army of the West gone, Halleck believed Curtis could capture Little Rock, the capital of Arkansas, with relative ease but this was not the case. One of the unintended consequences of Van Dorn's withdrawal was the emergence of guerrilla warfare in Arkansas. Confederate partisans, many of whom had deserted the Army of the West, waged a bloody campaign to protect their homeland from invasion, occupation, and subjugation. Confederate irregulars ambushed supply trains, harassed foraging parties, and executed captured Union soldiers. Despite a lack of centralized control, Arkansas guerrillas brought Curtis' advance to a standstill at Batesville, ninety miles north of Little Rock.

In May, the Confederate War Department gave the command of the Trans-Mississippi District to Maj. Gen. Thomas C. Hindman. A skilled administrator, Hindman had built a new Confederate force of some 12,000 troops, dubbed the Army of the Trans-Mississippi. Empowered by the Partisan Ranger Act, passed by the Confederate congress six weeks earlier, he immediately assembled various partisan units and small companies of volunteers to operate with little guidance and oversight. The added pressure from Hindman's rangers was more than Curtis' Northern army could endure. With Union lines of communications from Rolla in ruin, Curtis abandoned plans to reach Little Rock and instead turned his attention to Helena. Forced to live off the land, he implemented a policy of total war as he thundered down the White River, destroying everything in his path including civilian property.

As for Confederate partisans, Curtis characterized them as villainous assassins and authorized Union commanders to show no quarter. On 12 July, Curtis' Army of the Southwest took Helena and re-established supply lines with Federal forces on the Mississippi.

By June 1862, the Confederate War Department expanded General Hindman's authority to include the Department of the Trans-Mississippi, encompassing all Confederate territory west of the Mississippi River. Having foiled the Union offensive, he turned his attention to

General Hindman
(Library of Congress)

rebuilding a conventional force. His draconian approach, however, angered many in the Department, and in August, Richmond demoted Hindman to command of the Arkansas District and appointed Maj. Gen. Theophilus H. Holmes, a veteran of the regular Army, as commander of the Department of the Trans-Mississippi. Hindman persuaded Holmes to renew the offensive against Springfield by going on the offensive in Northwest Arkansas.

Reports of Confederate cavalry activity drew General Curtis' attention to southwest Missouri. He instructed Brig. Gen. John M. Schofield to secure the Missouri-Arkansas border and eliminate any Confederate force in the area. Schofield took the newly formed Army of the Frontier into the region and scattered the small force of Confederates there. He posted two divisions at Springfield and a third seventy-five miles south at Maysville, Arkansas. Complaining of illness, he returned to St. Louis, leaving Brig. Gen. James G. Blunt in command. Upon learning of Blunt's exposed position in Arkansas, Curtis advised him to fall back toward Springfield, but the counsel went unheeded.

In November, with the Army of the Trans-Mississippi concentrated at Fort Smith, Arkansas, Hindman seized what he saw as an opportunity to destroy the Union Army of the Frontier, starting with Blunt. He sent 2,000 cavalrymen under Brig. Gen. John S. Marmaduke to screen the Confederate advance. At the same time, Blunt pushed his 5,000-man division south to probe Confederate dispositions. The forces clashed on 28 November at Cane Hill. The Federals won a tactical victory, but Blunt's advanced position left him even more vulnerable and over one hundred miles from support. Still, after the fighting, he remained at Cane Hill. Blunt's decision was imprudent and needlessly put the security of his command and of southwest Missouri at risk.

On 3 December, Hindman moved to take advantage of Blunt's exposed position. His plan called for infantry to strike the force at Cane Hill, while cavalry rode east to gain the Federal rear and compel Blunt to surrender. Although Hindman's plan was technically sound, his army was ill prepared for the operation. Most of his men were green recruits or conscripts, and many shouldered inferior smoothbore muskets. Moreover, munitions and other supplies were insufficient to conduct the campaign effectively.

Meanwhile, Blunt sent word for Brig. Gen. Francis J. Herron, in command of two Union divisions in Springfield, to move his force south to Cane Hill at once. Herron led his 7,000 men on a forced march from Springfield, and arrived in Fayetteville before dawn on 7 December, having covered some 115 miles at a pace of over 35 miles per day. Hindman learned of Herron's advance on the night of 6 December but was not sure of his numerical strength. Nevertheless, he could not strike Blunt as planned with a Federal force in position to fall on his rear. He therefore decided to move east and attack Herron's command before it reached Cane Hill.

General Hindman moved his army to Prairie Grove, ten miles southwest of Fayetteville, and took up a defensive position on the hills overlooking the Illinois River and commanding the road to Cane Hill. When Herron's divisions arrived, the column came under fire from Confederate batteries on the ridge. Herron deployed his rifled guns along the Illinois River beyond reach of Confederate smoothbore cannon and destroyed Hindman's batteries. Federal infantry attacked the Confederate position, and throughout the morning, the armies struggled for control of the high ground. Meanwhile, at Cane Hill, Blunt remained unaware of Herron's predicament until the sounds of battle drew him toward Fayetteville. His Federals arrived at Prairie Grove after 1200, and attacked the Confederate left, just as Herron began to falter. Hindman repulsed Blunt's attack but could not exploit his advantage. As dusk approached, the battle came to an inconclusive end.

Hindman asked for a cease-fire to retrieve his casualties, and Blunt agreed. The truce was a ruse, however, and in the early hours of 8 December, Hindman withdrew his army to Fort Smith. During the retreat, many Confederates deserted, disillusioned with Hindman and the Confederacy. Blunt was furious and accused Hindman of unchivalrous conduct. He declared victory and, in late December, moved to take Van Buren and Fort Smith, both in northwest Arkansas. Hindman retreated south of the Arkansas River and then turned east toward Little Rock.

Although Prairie Grove ended as a tactical draw, it was another strategic Union victory. The battle decimated Hindman's army and thereby crippled the Confederacy's ability to wage an effective campaign for Missouri. Missouri and much of Arkansas would remain in Union hands for the rest of the war. The Federals held a firm grip on the area north of the Arkansas River from Indian Territory to the Mississippi River. In January 1863, they captured Fort Hindman, 117 miles southeast of Little Rock at Arkansas Post.

General Kirby Smith
(Library of Congress)

In September, Little Rock and Pine Bluff fell, and Union forces secured control of the Arkansas River Valley. These Union victories confined Southern forces to the southwest corner of the state.

For the Confederates, failure at Prairie Grove led to Hindman's transfer east and a shake-up in command for the Department of the Trans-Mississippi. Richmond reduced General Holmes to the Arkansas district command and appointed Lt. Gen. Edmund Kirby Smith to head the department. Kirby Smith was a West Point graduate and regular Army veteran, known across the South for his timely arrival at First Manassas, his organizational skills as a department commander in East Tennessee, and his role in the 1862 Kentucky Campaign.

The Red River Campaign: The Struggle for Louisiana and Texas

Along with St. Louis, New Orleans was a key component in the Union strategy to control the Mississippi River. Without control of the lower Mississippi and the Gulf Coast region, the United States could not project its military power in that sector of the Trans-Mississippi. The capture of New Orleans in April 1862 opened the door for the Union to push north from the mouth of the Mississippi while other Federal forces drove south along the river from Missouri, Arkansas, and Tennessee. At that time, the U. S. War Department began discussions regarding a campaign into Texas. Establishing a military presence in Texas would compel the Confederates to divert manpower from other theaters to meet the threat. Beyond that, the occupation of Texas would deprive Southern forces east of the Mississippi of an important source of food, animals, and raw materials.

Other voices also called for a Texas campaign. Many Northern politicians argued that the large German immigrant population in Texas would support the Union as volunteers for military service and as voters to re-establish a pro-Union state government. Economic and business interests also exerted pressure on the Lincoln administration to invade Texas. The Northern textile industry suffered from a cotton shortage that shuttered nearly three-quarters of the nation's mills and fueled both unemployment and inflation. To many Eastern industrialists, control of the Texas cotton fields held the solution to their economic woes. For all of these reasons, in October 1862, Secretary of War Edwin M. Stanton instructed Maj. Gen. Nathaniel P. Banks to prepare for an invasion of the Lone Star state.

General Banks
(Library of Congress)

On 14 December 1862, Banks arrived in New Orleans as commander of the Department of the Gulf. A former governor of Massachusetts and United States Congressman, Banks received the appointment for his political aptitude and not his military achievements. His orders were to secure the western side of the Mississippi River Valley, cooperate with General Grant in gaining control of the Mississippi River, and then turn toward Texas. To achieve these ends, General Banks commanded the XIX Corps with four divisions made up primarily of recent volunteers from New England and New York. Nearly half of the 42,000 troops under his command had enlisted for nine months, and few possessed any prior military experience. Banks deployed 40,000 troops in New Orleans for operations along the Mississippi, while the remainder garrisoned in Pensacola.

Banks directed most of his attention to developing a campaign along the Mississippi but felt beholden to the "on-to-Texas" contingent of politicians and cotton speculators that had accompanied him to New Orleans. Accordingly, he dispatched 300 men from the 42d Massachusetts Infantry to support a small Federal force that held a tenuous foothold in Galveston, Texas. The Confederates' Texas district commander, Maj. Gen. John B. Magruder, devised a two-pronged attack on the port city that called for approximately 1,000 dismounted cavalry troops to strike the Federal garrison by land while two cotton-clad gunboats, manned by 300 sharpshooters, slipped into Galveston Bay and engaged the six Union ships protecting the fortifications.

At dawn on New Year's Day 1863, Magruder's joint force struck the Union outpost. Although the overland attack failed, Confederate ships inflicted significant damage to their Union counterparts. With two Union gunboats crippled, the remainder of the warships steamed to safety in the Gulf. The outnumbered 42d Massachusetts surrendered, and the Confederates regained control of Galveston and the Texas coastline. For the moment, Union occupation of Texas would have to wait as Banks turned his focus to the reduction of Port Hudson, the Confederate fortress on the Mississippi between Baton Rouge and Vicksburg.

As Banks probed the avenues of advance from New Orleans to Port Hudson, a small Confederate force in south central Louisiana menaced his lines of communications. In the District of Western Louisiana, Maj. Gen. Richard Taylor commanded two Confederate divisions of Texans and Louisianans, many of whom were fighting in defense of their hometowns. The son of former United States President Zachary Taylor and brother-in-law of Confederate President Davis, Taylor had served as a brigadier general under "Stonewall" Jackson in the Shenandoah Valley. Recently transferred to district command in his home state, he engineered sorties that forced Banks to divert his attention from Port Hudson. Banks detached 16,000 men in two divisions and one brigade to clean the Bayou Teche region of Confederates in a campaign conducted from early April through late May 1863. The region was some sixty miles west of the Mississippi River in the south

General Taylor
(Library of Congress)

central portion of Louisiana, and the Bayou Teche flowed for 120 miles south from Opelousas to join the Atchafalaya River below Grand Lake, west of New Orleans.

By 9 April, the Federals reached Fort Bisland, the Confederate works west of Grand Lake on the Bayou Teche. Banks divided his force and, using naval transports on Grand Lake, forced Taylor's withdrawal from Fort Bisland. The Confederates moved up the bayou, deep into the Louisiana interior. The Federals pushed north all the way to Alexandria, just above the confluence of the Mississippi and the Red River.

In early May, as General Grant stepped up his campaign to take Vicksburg, Banks installed his army as an occupation force and began to probe the area beyond Alexandria for pathways into Texas. His foray deep into Louisiana concerned the Union high command. His army had already cleared Taylor's troops from the Teche region and, in doing so, had cut Port Hudson's supply line from the Louisiana interior. Banks' current operations, however, had little to do with his primary mission to clear the lower Mississippi, and from Washington, D.C., General in Chief of the U.S. Army Halleck called the activities at Alexandria "too eccentric to be pursued." He demanded that Banks move against Port Hudson immediately. On 14 May, Banks marched his command toward the Mississippi. By the time he arrived, one week later, he had concentrated 30,000 Federal troops against 7,500 Confederates at Port Hudson.

Despite the numerical discrepancy, the Confederate position was strong. The fortifications stretched across high ground, while the terrain surrounding the position was swampy and choked with thick underbrush that provided poor fields of fire and few avenues of advance for an attacking force. Moreover, interior lines allowed the talented Confederate commander, Maj. Gen. Franklin K. Gardner, to shift his troops and mass his firepower as needed. Banks devised a plan to offset Gardner's interior lines by ordering a simultaneous assault along the entire Confederate position. He assigned Brig. Gen. Thomas W. Sherman to lead the left wing and Brig. Gen. Godfrey Weitzel the right wing. Maj. Gen. Christopher C. Augur and Brig. Gen. Cuvier Grover would direct the attack against the Confederate center. Although Banks' subordinates disagreed on the wisdom of the plan, arguing instead for a siege, the commanding general insisted, "The people of the North want blood," and he ordered the attack to proceed.

On 27 May at 0530, Federal batteries and gunboats began shelling Port Hudson, but the infantry assault failed to unfold as planned. Weitzel's right wing moved against the northern flank of the Confederate line at 0600 but the terrain disrupted unit cohesion. Moreover, Union forces in the center and on the left failed to move in concert with the right wing, thus allowing Gardner to shift troops to meet each threat in turn. The Union left wing did not get under way until after 1200, and by then the Confederates had repulsed Weitzel's attack and secured the northern sector. The Union left wing thus faced a reinforced Confederate line, which the Federals were unable to break. Sherman fell wounded and was carried from the field. Similarly, at the center, Augur waited for direct orders to advance and did not move until after Sherman's repulse, while Grover's men did not advance until 1500. By then, the defenders had blunted the uncoordinated Union assault, and Banks broke off the fighting.

The Confederates counted fewer than 500 casualties, while Federal losses numbered over 2,000 and included some African American troops from the 1st and 3d Louisiana Native Guard organized in the fall of 1862. These regiments were in Col. John A. Nelson's brigade of Brig. Gen. William Dwight's division and saw action as part of the Union right wing.

Following the assaults of 27 May, General Banks settled in for a siege. On 14 June, he ordered an attack against a portion of the Confederate center at Fort Desperate but could not break the Southern lines. The Confederates held on at Port Hudson until receiving word that Vicksburg had fallen on 4 July. On 9 July, Port Hudson surrendered. With the Mississippi River in Union hands, Banks returned his attention to Texas.

By the summer of 1863, a new development added to the urgency of the Texas mission. French Emperor Napoleon III had invaded Mexico in 1861, and in June 1863, his troops captured Mexico City. Rumblings of a possible Franco-Confederate alliance worried the Lincoln administration. Union control of Texas would do much to dissuade the French from aiding the Confederates, and the conquest of Texas was therefore of increasing importance to President Lincoln.

General Banks examined a variety of invasion routes and favored an amphibious landing on the Gulf Coast over a campaign through the Louisiana interior. In August, he devised a plan to move elements of the XIX Corps on naval transports to Sabine Pass, a lightly defended position on the Gulf at the border of

Texas and Louisiana. Once the Federals gained control of the pass, they would use the area as a staging ground for a full-scale invasion of Texas, while the Navy protected supply lines on the Gulf and up the Sabine River.

Banks gave Maj. Gen. William B. Franklin command of the expedition. Franklin was a West Point graduate whose lackluster performance at Fredericksburg in 1862 had earned him a transfer to the Trans-Mississippi. Nonetheless, with elements of the XIII Corps arriving in New Orleans, ostensibly to replace troops whose enlistments had recently

General Franklin
(Library of Congress)

expired, Banks reorganized the XIX Corps and gave Franklin the command. On 4 September, an invasion force of 5,000 bluecoats boarded transports and, accompanied by several gunboats, set out for the Sabine Pass.

On 7 September, the flotilla reached the pass without incident, but the following day brought disaster. Confederate Lt. Richard W. "Dick" Dowling, a young Irish immigrant, held the position with just forty-two men, mostly Irish-born Texans, and twelve guns. Dowling's artillery controlled the channel, and it decimated the Union force, disabling 2 ships and inflicting 375 casualties, while the Confederates did not lose a single man. Franklin abandoned the mission and returned to New Orleans. Texas district commander General Magruder called Dowling's performance "the most extraordinary feat of the war."

After the fiasco at Sabine Pass, Banks designed overlapping operations for Texas and Louisiana. In October 1863, he ordered General Franklin into the Teche region with instructions to advance to Opelousas, the temporary Confederate capital of Louisiana. Once Franklin reached that point, the Federals could continue to move northwest and reach Texas by way of the Red River, or turn west and strike for the Sabine River. Franklin's column moved cautiously as enemy cavalry slashed at its flanks and rear. When the outnumbered Confederates offered battle near Opelousas, Franklin ordered a retreat.

At the same time, Banks sent another amphibious expedition to Brownsville, Texas. Across the Rio Grande from Matamoras, Brownsville was a trade center for cotton, munitions, and medicine. The 2d Division of the XIII Corps took Brownsville on 6 November and installed Andrew Jackson Hamilton, a Texas Unionist, as provisional governor. The Federals now controlled the lower Rio Grande valley from Brownsville up to Laredo but failed to shut down illicit trade or win over civilians to the Union occupation. In the spring of 1864, General Magruder sent Col. John Salmon "Rip" Ford to retake the lower Rio Grande Valley. Ford was a former Texas Ranger and politician, who forged a colorful collection of state troops, conscripts, home guard, deserters, partisans, outlaws, and civilians, ranging from teenagers to old men, into his self-styled Cavalry of the West. Urging his men to defend their homes against the "mongrel force" of Union invaders, Ford inched his 1,800-man force south from San Antonio toward Laredo and then east toward Brownsville. In late June, a 400-man Confederate reconnaissance force clashed with Union troops outside of Brownsville. Ford learned that fewer than half of the 6,000 Union troops remained at Fort Brown. For three weeks, he prepared to attack the fort, but in late July, he learned that the Federals had evacuated Brownsville.

General Steele
(National Archives)

Meanwhile, General Halleck started to pressure Banks to invade Texas through Louisiana along the Red River. Halleck promised to provide Banks with support from Maj. Gen. Frederick Steele's Army of Arkansas and from Maj. Gen. William T. Sherman's Army of the Tennessee. In addition, President Lincoln endorsed a Red River campaign, in part because Banks could use Louisiana as a laboratory for the administration's reconstruction policy. Banks consented and, with Halleck's direction, began to draw up plans for the campaign.

The Army of the Gulf would provide most of the manpower for the expedition with over 18,000 men under Banks' command. General Franklin would lead the XIX Corps with Brig. Gen. William H. Emory's 1st Division and Brig. Gen. Albert L. Lee's Cavalry Division. Brig. Gen. Thomas E. G. Ransom would command a detachment from the XIII Corps that included the 3d Division under Brig. Gen. Robert A. Cameron and the 4th Division under Col. William J. Landram. The expedition would draw on an additional 11,000 men from the XVI and XVII Corps of the Army of the Tennessee. Brig. Gen. Andrew Jackson Smith, a Pennsylvanian, West Point graduate, and regular Army veteran, led this contingent that included two divisions from the XVI Corps, the 1st and 3d under the command of Brig. Gen. Joseph A. Mower, along with a provisional division from the XVII Corps, designated as the 2d Division under Brig. Gen. Thomas Kilby Smith. Joining A. J. Smith's command was Brig. Gen. Alfred W. Ellet's Mississippi Marine Brigade.

General A. J. Smith
(National Archives)

Banks planned a massive pincer movement directed at Shreveport, Louisiana, the new capital of the Confederate Trans-Mississippi and the department's industrial center. The XIX and XIII Corps would march from Baton Rouge to Alexandria; there they would unite with General A. J. Smith's forces. Admiral David D. Porter's fleet of warships would accompany these troops to Alexandria. Porter's fleet, the largest ever assembled on North American waters, totaled 104 vessels and included an array of ironclads, tinclads, river monitors, and transports. Once united at Alexandria, Banks, A. J. Smith, and Porter would advance northwest along the Red River to Shreveport with the navy providing logistical support as well as firepower. At Shreveport, the Louisiana arm of the campaign would rendezvous with 11,000 troops from Arkansas under General Steele. This force consisted of the 3d Division of Steele's VII Corps, a total of 7,000 men, and another 4,000 soldiers from the Army of the Frontier under Brig. Gen. John M. Thayer. Steele and Thayer would unite their forces in the southwest corner of the state at Arkadelphia, the former marching southwest from Little Rock and the latter marching south from Fort Smith. From Arkadelphia, they would continue on to Shreveport and a junction with Banks' army. Once in Shreveport, a portion of Banks' force would march west into Texas, while the remainder occupied the city.

The plan suffered from poor design with too many elements left to chance. While Banks stipulated Shreveport as the objective, he never clearly defined or prioritized the military, political, and economic goals for the campaign. He certainly hoped to take the offensive against enemy forces that totaled less than one-third of his numbers, but he did not specify the destruction of the Confederate army in Louisiana as the primary objective. Moreover, Banks would not achieve concentration until he reached Shreveport. The multifaceted operation called for precise coordination and communication between columns separated by hundreds of miles. Worse yet for Banks, the Northern press published the particulars of the invasion plans, and Confederate operatives in New Orleans provided detailed information of the operation to General Taylor. The lack of security eliminated the element of surprise. This gave the Confederates an opportunity to utilize interior lines to gain a tactical advantage at a time and place of their choosing.

Internal divisions further jeopardized the Union plans. While the campaign included units from four different armies and from the navy, General Halleck failed to appoint a single individual to direct the action. General William T. Sherman had offered to oversee operations, but Banks outranked him, and Sherman refused to serve under an officer of dubious military talent. As a result, Sherman sent General A. J. Smith to lead the contingent from the Army of the Tennessee. In Arkansas, General Steele was unenthusiastic about the campaign. He sought to exert his authority by continually making unilateral decisions regarding the disposition of his command and the prosecution of the campaign.

The navy added to the internal dissention as Admiral Porter considered himself exempt from orders, instructions, or suggestions issued by any army officer, particularly from a nonprofessional like Banks. General Grant specified that A. J. Smith's troops were on loan and that Banks must return them to the Army of the Tennessee by 15 April, thus creating an arbitrary deadline for the capture of Shreveport.

Admiral Porter
(Library of Congress)

Beset by a host of problems, the campaign got underway on 7 March 1864, one week behind schedule, when Lee's 5,000 Union cavalry troopers rode out from Baton Rouge, headed for Alexandria. A. J. Smith's Federals left Vicksburg on 10 March and, along with Porter's fleet, entered the Red River two days later. The lead column of Banks' infantry, commanded by General Franklin, set off on 15 March. The Federals in Arkansas did not begin until 21 March, nearly three weeks behind schedule.

The Red River Expedition, Louisiana and Texas, 1864
(Library of Congress)

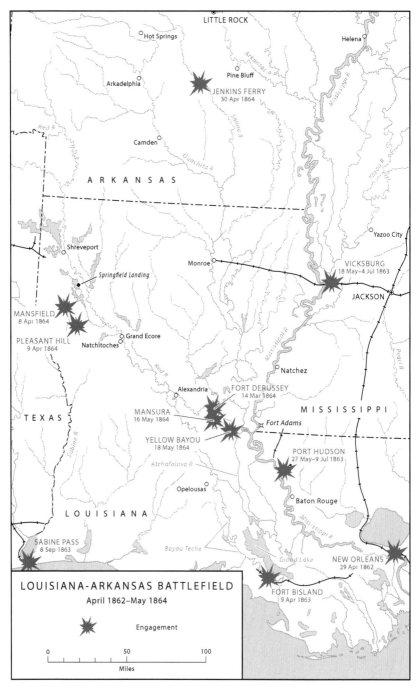

LITTLE ROCK

Hot Springs

Helena

Pine Bluff

Arkadelphia

JENKINS FERRY
30 Apr 1864

Camden

A R K A N S A S

Yazoo City

Shreveport

Monroe

VICKSBURG
18 May–4 Jul 1863

JACKSON

Springfield Landing

MANSFIELD
8 Apr 1864

Grand Ecore

PLEASANT HILL
9 Apr 1864

Natchitoches

Natchez

Alexandria

FORT DERUSSEY
14 Mar 1864

T E X A S

MANSURA
16 May 1864

M I S S I S S I P P I

Fort Adams

YELLOW BAYOU
18 May 1864

PORT HUDSON
27 May–9 Jul 1863

Atchafalaya R.

Opelousas

Baton Rouge

L O U I S I A N A

SABINE PASS
8 Sep 1863

Bayou Teche

Grand Lake

NEW ORLEANS
29 Apr 1862

FORT BISLAND
9 Apr 1863

LOUISIANA-ARKANSAS BATTLEFIELD

April 1862–May 1864

Engagement

0   50   100

Miles

MAP 6

Confederate agents apprised General Kirby Smith of the Union campaign in January, and he ordered Trans-Mississippi district commanders to prepare. Troops in Indian Territory gathered along the Arkansas border, while those in Texas moved toward the Louisiana line. In Arkansas, Price, recently elevated to district command and the rank of major general, had 14,000 troops. He deployed his cavalry above Camden, while Brig. Gen. Thomas Churchill held the town with his own division of Arkansas infantry and Brig. Gen. Mosby Parson's division of Missourians. Kirby Smith ordered General Taylor to dam the Red River upstream by sinking the 300-foot steamer *New Falls City*, and wedging bow and stern into opposite riverbanks. Downstream, Taylor's men refurbished a series of forts and water batteries, the most prominent of which, Fort DeRussy, stood between the mouth of the Red River and Alexandria (*Map 6*).

General Kirby Smith ordered Taylor and Price to retard the Federal advance but to avoid a general engagement and fall back toward Shreveport. By using interior lines, Kirby Smith hoped to mass his forces at a central position for a strike against whichever arm of the Federal pincer presented the more immediate threat to the capital. Then, he would turn and concentrate against the other Federal column. While this plan was sound, given the numerical discrepancy that Kirby Smith faced, it required Taylor and Price to retreat in the face of the enemy, and neither district commander endorsed the strategy.

On 13 March, the Federal vanguard ascended the Red River. The next day the joint Federal force advanced fifteen miles up river to the Confederate works at Fort DeRussy. Porter's gunships began to shell the fort while A. J. Smith deployed the 1st and 2d Brigades of the 1st Division, XVI Corps, into line of battle to take the rebel defenses from the rear. Confederate Maj. Gen. John G. Walker prepared to contest the Federal advance along the Marksville Road, but citing the discrepancy in strength and firepower, fell back without a fight, and Fort DeRussy surrendered before the Union assault began. The battle was little more than a skirmish, with the Federals suffering 38 casualties while capturing 310 Confederates, 10 guns, and a supply of ordnance. With the lower Red River in Federal hands, the path to Alexandria lay open. Taylor abandoned the town and moved upriver toward Natchitoches.

General Banks did not reach Alexandria until 25 March, ten days after the first Federal troops had entered the town. He and Admiral Porter faced significant challenges. The anticipated seasonal rise in the water level of the Red River above Alexandria had failed to materialize. This meant that most vessels in Porter's fleet could not continue upriver, leaving Banks without logistical support. Under pressure from Grant to take Shreveport by 15 April, Porter managed to get thirteen gunboats and thirty transports above the falls at Alexandria on the Red River. On 26 March, advance elements of Banks' column moved toward Natchitoches, where they arrived on 30 March.

At Natchitoches, General Banks' staff failed to locate the road that ran alongside the Red River to Shreveport. Rather than spend additional time reconnoitering, Banks chose to have his men take the stagecoach road that ran inland, away from the river and from the protection of the Union fleet. Porter would continue upriver while Banks marched across country through Mansfield. Once past Mansfield, the army and navy would reunite at Springfield Landing, just below Shreveport, and reach their objective ahead of General Grant's 15 April deadline. Banks' troops began the march on 6 April, while Porter began to steam for Springfield Landing the following day. Banks based his decision in part on misleading intelligence from locals, as well as the lack of resistance from Confederate forces. Certainly pressure from Grant to return A. J. Smith's troops to the Army of the Tennessee also influenced Banks. Nevertheless, the decision proved a costly mistake that changed the course of the campaign.

The stagecoach road was narrow, at some points no more than a ditch that snaked its way through pine forests that pressed in from both sides. The march progressed slowly with Lee's Union cavalry in the lead. Franklin's troops followed, strung out for twenty miles, with A. J. Smith's command slogging through the mud left in Franklin's wake.

Lee ran into Brig. Gen. Thomas Green's veteran Texas cavalry at Wilson's farm, twenty miles south of Mansfield. Recognizing that he faced more than token enemy resistance, Lee brought up his artillery to drive off the Confederates and sent word to Franklin for support. He eventually received the 1st Brigade, some 1,200 men, of Landram's division of the XIII Corps.

On the evening of 7 April, after a council of war, General Taylor determined that the Federal order of march combined with the wooded terrain and the narrow road reduced Banks' ability to rapidly concentrate his superior firepower. On the other hand, once past Mansfield, the road divided into three parallel avenues of advance, with one road running to the river at Springfield Landing. This would allow Banks to move his army along separate roads, each within supporting distance of one another, and enable his infantry to re-establish contact with the fleet. Taylor concluded that if the Federals passed Mansfield, Shreveport would certainly fall. Consequently, he decided to disregard General Kirby Smith's orders to fall back toward a concentration of forces at Shreveport and to take the offensive south of Mansfield.

Taylor selected the Moss plantation three miles below the town to confront the Federal advance. There, the road emerged from the woods on Honeycutt Hill and ran northwest across an open field that measured 1,200 yards in length and 800 yards in width. Taylor planned to deploy infantry across the road and use the woods north of the field to conceal his cavalry on the flanks. He hoped to draw Banks down from Honeycutt Hill and into the open where the Confederate infantry would drive the Federals back on their trains while Confederate cavalry enveloped the flanks.

Col. Frank Emerson's Federal brigade, accompanied by Colonel Landram, reached General Lee's cavalry camp at Carroll's Mill early on the morning of 8 April and the cavalry promptly renewed the advance. The Federals drove Confederate skirmishers through woods for six miles until they reached the clearing below the northwest slope of Honeycutt Hill. There, across the field, Lee saw Taylor's force deployed into line of battle. Lee positioned his troopers in a defensive alignment along the crest of Honeycutt Hill and sent word to General Franklin for infantry support. Franklin instructed Ransom to bring up the 2d Brigade of the 4th Division, and General Banks rode to the front to assess the situation. Banks arrived around 1300 and sent word for Franklin to bring up the remainder of his force at once. The commanding general instructed Lee to hold his position until support arrived.

Lee skirmished with the Confederates throughout the afternoon as Union support came to the front, slowed by the narrow road and the wooded terrain. By 1530, Landram's 4th Division was in position with Col. Joseph W. Vance's brigade to the right of the road and Emerson's brigade astride the road. Capt. Ormand F. Nims' 2d Massachusetts battery took a position in the center of the road while the Chicago Mercantile battery, under Lt. Pinkney S. Cone, unlimbered its guns northeast of the road on the slope of Honeycutt Hill. The Federals positioned cavalry on the flanks with

Col. Thomas J. Lucas' brigade securing the right and Col. Nathan A. M. Dudley's brigade anchoring the left. Altogether, the Federals had 5,000 men.

Nearly 1,000 yards across the field, Taylor had deployed Brig. Gen. J. Alfred Mouton's division to the left of the Mansfield Road and posted Walker's Texans to the right with elements of Green's cavalry holding each flank and artillery manning the center. Taylor had 8,800 effectives and outnumbered the Federals, but the Federals remained atop Honeycutt Hill in a defensive posture, and with each passing hour they grew in strength as reinforcements arrived at the front. Taylor had to take the initiative or risk losing the battle and the campaign. At 1600, he ordered Mouton to attack.

On the Confederate left, Mouton's division charged across the field and up the slope of Honeycutt Hill northeast of the Mansfield Road. To their front, General Ransom's five Union regiments commanded the field from a strong position behind a split rail fence. Two hundred yards from the Federal line, advancing Confederates reached a swale and paused to re-form. General Mouton rode among his men to rally the troops, and they soon renewed the assault. As Mouton's division closed on the Federal right, Taylor sent Walker's division against the left. Walker's Texans struck the line and battled for control of the Union guns on the Mansfield Road. General Ransom pulled the 83d Ohio Infantry from the right flank and sent them to rescue the battery but by the time the regiment arrived, the Texans had broken the Union left, seized the battery, and turned the guns on the Federals.

Confederates swarmed across the crest of Honeycutt Hill and the Union line collapsed. Ransom was wounded, and brigade commanders Emerson and Vance were wounded and taken prisoner. Without leaders to steady the men and direct the retreat, Federal discipline disintegrated. Confederates cut off the 48th Ohio Infantry and 130th Illinois Infantry and nearly annihilated these regiments. Meanwhile, the remaining Union soldiers fell back through the woods until they met General Cameron and the 3d Division of the XIII Corps, accompanied by General Franklin. The Federals re-formed with the remnants of some cavalry, as Franklin sent an order to General Emory to bring up the XIX Corps and form a defensive line to the rear of the XIII Corps, lest the enemy force another retreat. In less than an hour, the Union line began to break again. General Banks arrived as the line gave way and could not rally the panicked troops. Soldiers became entangled with the trains, and Confederate cavalry enveloped the flanks, gobbling up prisoners and shooting men as they fled. General Franklin suffered a leg wound and barely escaped capture.

Around 1800, the retreating Federals reached Emory's deployed XIX Corps at Pleasant Grove, two miles below the Moss Plantation. The Confederates approached, but the day's fighting left them too disorganized for another coordinated assault.

The Battle of Mansfield, also called Sabine Crossroads, cost Banks 2,200 casualties out of 12,000 engaged while Taylor lost 1,000 men of his 8,800. Among Taylor's losses was General Mouton, who was killed on Honeycutt Hill after the Federals had begun their retreat. Mouton had spotted a group of isolated Federal soldiers from the 19th Kentucky Infantry who had thrown down their arms and surrendered. As he rode forward to investigate, several of the men picked up their weapons and shot him. Nearby Confederates who witnessed the event rushed the Federals and killed them.

At Pleasant Grove, General Banks held a council of war and, at the urging of his generals, ordered a withdrawal to Pleasant Hill, a village on a slight plateau nearly fourteen miles to the southeast. There, the army would regroup and, with the support of A. J. Smith's XVI Corps bluecoats, take a defensive position and await Taylor's next move. A. J. Smith posted his command south of the town along a low ridge. The XIII Corps had suffered the brunt of the attack at

The Battle of Pleasant Hill
(Library of Congress)

Mansfield, and Banks sent them to the rear while he posted Emory's 1st Division from the XIX Corps on the north side of Pleasant Hill. Emory sent Col. William T. Shaw's brigade, detached from the XVI Corps, to hold the Mansfield Road north of town with General Dwight's brigade east of the road and Col. Lewis Benedict's brigade farther west along the Sabine River Road. Brig. Gen. James W. McMillan's brigade was in reserve behind Dwight.

The position was poor and the deployments questionable. Shaw was far ahead of Dwight and Benedict, and thus his flanks were exposed. Dwight's left ran at an angle from the Mansfield Road behind Shaw, while his right bent back toward McMillan's reserves. Benedict was over 300 yards to Shaw's rear and concealed by woods. Meanwhile, Smith's corps held the Jessup Road from Natchitoches at least 300 yards behind Benedict's left. General Banks did not anticipate the coming battle. In fact, he planned to resume the advance on Shreveport that evening, which may account for the carelessness with which he positioned his army.

At 0900, Confederate cavalry found the Federals in line of battle at Pleasant Hill. Reconnaissance reported Emory's position in front of the town but failed to uncover the presence of the XVI Corps posted to the rear. Thus, Taylor based his plan of attack on incomplete intelligence. He planned to envelop Banks' left flank first. Once he did so, other Confederate units would strike the Union center while his cavalry enveloped the Federal right and cut off avenues of retreat to the river.

At 1630, twelve Confederate guns posted astride the Mansfield Road opened on Shaw's brigade, 800 yards away, initiating an artillery duel that shattered the afternoon calm. Thirty minutes later, as Shaw's guns fell silent, General Churchill's Confederate division roared into action on the Federal left. The Confederates then struck the Union center, and Taylor's cavalrymen, seeing the Union line begin to give way, charged the right. The attack, however, was poorly executed. Although the Southerners gained some success against Banks' center, A. J. Smith's XVI Corps hit the Confederates hard and unhinged the enemy attack. The Confederates fell back in disorder as darkness encroached.

The Battle of Pleasant Hill ended with Banks' army sustaining 1,400 casualties and Taylor's force losing 1,700, with each side having some 12,000 engaged. Taylor faulted himself for failing to oversee the details in his troops' dispositions. Banks credited

A. J. Smith with the victory and personally rode to congratulate him after the battle: "God bless you general, you have saved the army."

That night, Banks called a council of war. Generals Franklin, Emory, and Dwight all urged him to pull back to the river, where the army could resupply and reorganize under the protection of the fleet. Then, after a few days, the army would resume the march to Shreveport. Banks concurred and ordered a retreat to Grand Ecore. General A. J. Smith was not at the meeting but upon learning of the decision, protested and insisted Banks give him time to collect his wounded and bury his dead. When Banks declined, A. J. Smith petitioned Franklin to arrest the commanding general. Franklin refused, and the Army of the Gulf began its retreat. While Pleasant Hill was a tactical victory for the Federals, Banks' decision to retreat turned the battle into a strategic win for the Confederates.

Immediately following Pleasant Hill, General Taylor met with the department commander. With Banks in retreat, Kirby Smith wanted Taylor to march to Arkansas to secure the northern front. Taylor maintained that once the Federals in Arkansas learned of Banks' retreat, General Steele would abandon his operations and return to Little Rock. He beseeched Kirby Smith to allow him to destroy the Federals in Louisiana, but the commanding general refused. Without confirmation that Steele was in retreat, Kirby Smith could not risk leaving Shreveport vulnerable to the column advancing from the north. On 12 April, he sent two-thirds of Taylor's army on a forced march to join General Price in Arkansas and stop Steele. Kirby Smith planned to ride to Arkansas to join the Confederate force and personally lead them in battle. Before leaving for Arkansas, he told Taylor that if Steele retreated, he would indeed return the troops to Louisiana. Until then, only Green's cavalry and Brig. Gen. Camille Polignac's infantry division remained with Taylor for operations against Banks and Porter.

The Federals at Grand Ecore did not realize that Taylor was left with just a skeleton force of barely 5,000 men. Indeed, Banks believed that Taylor had him pinned down with 25,000 troops. For six days, Banks contemplated the situation and weighed his options. During that time he reorganized the army. He replaced his chief of staff, Brig. Gen. Charles P. Stone, with General Dwight, and relieved his cavalry commander, Lee, replacing him with Brig. Gen. Richard Arnold, formerly the chief of artillery. These moves indicated that Banks sought to shift blame for the failure to reach Shreveport to subordinates. Although Banks considered resuming the march on Shreveport, Admiral Porter insisted that, with the water level continuing to fall, the navy could not move upriver. In addition, Banks was under increasing pressure from Grant to return the XVI Corps to General Sherman's army. With these factors in mind, Banks ordered a retreat, and the army arrived at Alexandria on 23 April.

On 27 April, Porter's fleet finally arrived at Alexandria after a harrowing journey downriver. By the time the flotilla arrived, the river had fallen to four feet in places, far less than the seven feet needed to pass the town and enter the river below. The Confederates encircled the city as Porter struggled to find a solution to his predicament. General Banks could not remain at Alexandria indefinitely, and yet, without infantry protection, the navy risked losing the fleet. The solution came from Lt. Col. Joseph Bailey, an engineer on General Franklin's staff. Bailey suggested construction of a series of wing dams to span the river and raise the water level enough for the ships to move into the lower Red. Banks and Porter approved the project, and on 8 May, elements of the flotilla began to cross over the falls. By 13 May, the last of the ships steamed into the lower Red River. For his engineering feat, Bailey received a promotion to brigadier general and won the Medal of Honor.

With Porter gone, Banks ordered Alexandria abandoned, and A. J. Smith's troops proceeded to fire the town. By then, Banks had lost control over A. J. Smith and was powerless to stop the destruction. General Taylor pursued the retiring Federals, battling them on 16 May at Mansura and again on 18 May at Yellow Bayou, before the Union army escaped across the Mississippi River, ending the Red River campaign.

The campaign was a strategic defeat for the Federals, who failed to accomplish any of their objectives. While General Banks won several tactical victories, his resounding defeat at Mansfield ultimately proved the decisive contest of the campaign. Banks' personal courage and determination could not compensate for his weak leadership and lack of sound judgment. In all, Banks lost 5,400 men along with 20 guns, 200 wagons, and 1,000 horses, while Porter lost 9 ships and suffered 300 casualties. Confederate losses totaled 4,000.

Taylor's superior generalship was the deciding factor. Not only did he inspire his subordinates and his troops, but his use and selection of terrain enabled the ragged Confederate army to win a campaign against a force three times its size. In doing so, the

Confederates saved the political and industrial center at Shreveport, defended the fertile Red River valley, and secured Texas.

Taylor insisted that he could have annihilated Banks' army and captured Porter's fleet if not for Kirby Smith's decision to take two-thirds of the infantry to Arkansas. As Taylor had predicted, General Steele retreated upon learning of Banks' defeat. This meant that Shreveport was safe, but rather than sending Confederate infantry back to Taylor, Kirby Smith had pursued Steele's Federals. On 30 April, while Banks and Porter languished at Alexandria, Kirby Smith caught Steele at Jenkins Ferry, along the Saline River. The inconclusive battle at Jenkins Ferry left the Confederates with one thousand casualties, while the Federals suffered half that number. Strategically, the battle accomplished nothing for the Confederates as the Federals continued their retreat to Little Rock.

Throughout the campaign, Taylor had protested Kirby Smith's Fabian policy of strategic retreat. Once the campaign ended, Taylor stepped up his criticism to the point of insubordination. Kirby Smith relieved him from command and appointed General Walker to district command. Within weeks, the Confederate government promoted Taylor to lieutenant general and gave him command of the Department of Mississippi, Alabama, and East Louisiana. Banks, too, was relieved of command and replaced by Maj. Gen. Edward R. S. Canby, who commanded the newly formed Division of West Mississippi that absorbed the Department of the Gulf and the Department of Arkansas. Banks remained in New Orleans to implement the Unionist state government that he helped install during the preceding months.

Price's Missouri Raid

Although Banks' campaign failed, a positive but unintended consequence of operations along the Red River for the Union was the disruption of Confederate designs for the Trans-Mississippi. General Kirby Smith had planned to lead the South's Army of the Trans-Mississippi into Missouri. Indeed, before the Federals launched the Red River Campaign, Kirby Smith had believed that Taylor could hold western Louisiana with a small force while the bulk of the army reclaimed Arkansas, liberated Missouri, and captured St. Louis. The Federal invasion through the Red River Valley had forced Kirby Smith to shift to the defensive in Louisiana and by the time the campaign ended, the Army of the

Trans-Mississippi was too weak to initiate offensive operations into Arkansas and Missouri.

During the summer, Kirby Smith met with General Price and Thomas C. Reynolds, the Confederate governor of Missouri, to discuss options for the state. In lieu of a full-scale invasion, Kirby Smith sent Price on a cavalry raid into Missouri with St. Louis as the objective. Once Price seized the city, the Confederates believed that as many as 20,000 volunteers would flock to the colors. This would force the Federals to divert troops from other theaters to battle the Confederates for control of Missouri.

On 19 September, Price led 12,000 men across the Arkansas line and into Missouri. His newly formed Army of Missouri consisted of three divisions, led by General Marmaduke, Maj. Gen. James F. Fagan, and the flamboyant Brig. Gen. Joseph O. Shelby. The army contained men from Missouri and Arkansas and included several veteran units, but nearly one-third of Price's force consisted of untrained, inexperienced, and ill-equipped conscripts. (*See Map 7.*)

On 25 September, the Confederates approached Fort Davidson, sixty-five miles south of St. Louis. The fort was a hexagonal series of earthworks and rifle pits ringed by a dry moat, ten feet in width with a depth of six feet. The commander of the District of St. Louis, Brig. Gen. Thomas Ewing Jr., had 1,500 men at the fort, although only 900 were fit for duty.

Fort Davidson stood in the Acadian Valley, blocking the Confederate route to St. Louis and creating a dilemma for Price. Shelby urged him to bypass the fort and push on to St. Louis, but Fagan and Marmaduke argued in favor of reducing the garrison before going ahead. Despite instructions from Kirby Smith to move rapidly to St. Louis, Price chose to attack the outpost. Marmaduke and Fagan would

General Ewing
(National Archives)

52

assault the fort while Shelby cut Federal lines of communications. The decision marked the turning point of the campaign.

Price planned to put his guns along Pilot Knob and Shepherd's Mountain, two ridges that ringed the Federal position. From there, the batteries could direct fire into the fort and compel the Federals to surrender. Before hostilities commenced, however, Price received word that General Ewing held a group of Confederate sympathizers as prisoners inside the post. If the guns opened fire, the civilians would suffer the consequences. Fagan and Marmaduke proposed a change in tactics with artillery supporting a frontal attack. Although this would expose Confederate troops to Federal fire as they advanced 900 yards across the open valley floor, Price's lieutenants insisted that superior numbers would enable them to carry the works with minimal casualties. Price approved the plan but cautioned that his divisions must move in concert.

On 27 September, the Confederates opened the attack. Federal artillery held superior fields of fire, and Ewing's twelve guns extracted a heavy toll. Moreover, Price and his commanders failed to anticipate the effect that the terrain would have on the troops. The broken ground disrupted unit cohesion, and the charge degenerated into a series of piecemeal assaults. Many of the green Confederates broke and ran, while veteran units took heavy casualties. Numerous Confederates who reached the fort were hit by Ketchum grenades, concussion devices that the Federals lobbed over the walls and down onto the attackers. When the Confederates fell back, Price counted 1,000 casualties while Ewing lost 200 men.

The following day, Price considered renewing the attack, and the Confederates constructed ladders to scale the walls of the fort, but Ewing had withdrawn before dawn. Even so, Price could not declare victory. The battle had been a disaster for his army and for his mission. He had underestimated Ewing and approved a battle plan that failed to exploit the relative strengths and weaknesses of the opposing positions. To add to the sting of defeat, Shelby failed to secure a position across the Federal line of retreat, and Ewing escaped to St. Louis. Initially, Price planned a pursuit, but Shelby reported that A. J. Smith's Union XVI Corps was advancing toward the Confederates. This intelligence, combined with the defeat at Pilot Knob, prompted Price to abandon plans for St. Louis and turn the columns west toward Jefferson City.

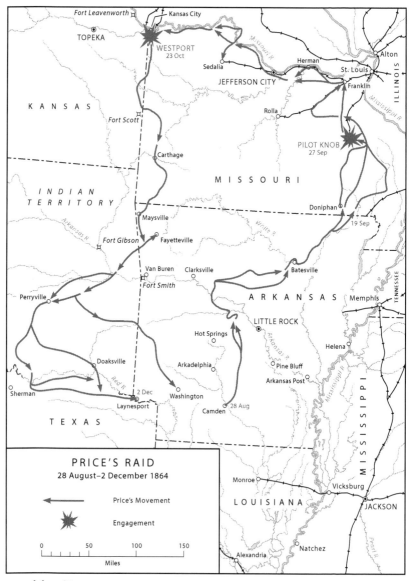

Fort Leavenworth Kansas City
TOPEKA
WESTPORT
23 Oct
Sedalia Herman St. Louis Alton
ILLINOIS
JEFFERSON CITY Franklin
K A N S A S
Fort Scott
Rolla
PILOT KNOB
27 Sep
Carthage
I N D I A N
T E R R I T O R Y
Doniphan
Maysville 19 Sep
White R.
Fort Gibson Fayetteville
Arkansas R.
Van Buren Clarksville Batesville
Fort Smith
Perryville A R K A N S A S Memphis
TENNESSEE
Hot Springs LITTLE ROCK
Doaksville Helena
Arkadelphia Pine Bluff
Red R. Arkansas Post
Sherman 2 Dec Washington
Laynesport Camden 28 Aug M I S S I S S I P P I
T E X A S

PRICE'S RAID
28 August–2 December 1864

⟵   Price's Movement

✸   Engagement

Monroe Vicksburg
L O U I S I A N A JACKSON

0   50   100   150
Miles

Alexandria Natchez

MAP 7

Price picked up 7,000 recruits along the way, but discipline problems plagued his efforts to sway Missourians to the Confederate cause. In fact, rampant looting of towns and villages by the Confederates had the opposite effect. Straggling also beset the march as Price moved through the state at a laggardly pace. This gave the Union commander of the Department of Missouri, Maj. Gen. William S. Rosecrans, and his cavalry chief, Maj. Gen. Alfred Pleasanton, time to coordinate pursuit of the southern column. As Pleasanton's cavalry and A. J. Smith's infantry chased Price from the east, General Curtis gathered his troops from the Department of Kansas to intercept the Confederate column from the west. Price skirmished his way across Missouri until 22 October, when he reached Westport, just south of Kansas City.

At a council of war that night, Price considered moving toward Kansas City or Leavenworth, Kansas. However, intelligence reports revealed Curtis' Army of the Border massed to the west with 10,000 soldiers. In addition, Pleasanton's cavalry, also with 10,000 men, was closing in from the east. Although outnumbered three-to-one, Price realized that U.S. forces were divided, and he hoped to destroy each in detail. Price planned to take two divisions and strike Curtis' force along the Brush Creek south of Westport, while a third rebel division delayed Pleasanton's advance at the Big Blue River to the east. Upon defeating Curtis, Price would turn and concentrate his force against Pleasanton. If successful, this would allow the Confederates unencumbered entrance into Kansas.

In the predawn hours of 23 October, Union General Blunt seized the initiative and sent two brigades across the Brush Creek to engage Price's divisions. The fighting swayed back and forth along the ridges and through open fields until Confederate General Shelby's Iron Brigade drove the Federals back across the Brush Creek. A lack of ammunition and concern over a threat from Pleasanton, who was now engaged, prevented the Confederates from pressing their advantage and they remained south of the creek. This gave the Federals time to regroup and resume the offensive, but a second assault also failed to dislodge the rebels. Curtis sought to avoid another frontal attack and enlisted the aid of a local farmer in locating an avenue of approach to the Confederate left. Leading his own escort and the 9th Wisconsin Battery through a ravine along the Swan Creek, Curtis took position directly on Shelby's left flank. As Curtis' artillery tore through the Confederate flank, Blunt resumed the attack against the rebel center. With fresh troops at his disposal, including Kansas militia in support, Blunt began to unravel the rebel defenses. Moreover, to the east, Pleasanton's command had fought its way across the Big Blue River. Marmaduke's division grudgingly gave way and fell back toward the main Confederate position below Westport.

Once elements of Pleasanton's command reached Westport, Price came under fire on three sides. Fearing encirclement, he had little choice but to withdraw and, in doing so, to abandon the campaign. The Battle of Westport cost each side 1,500 soldiers.

The Federals gave chase, but fierce rear guard actions secured the Confederate retreat that carried Price southwest through Indian Territory, before the army finally crossed the Red River and entered Texas. From there Price turned east and reached Laynesport, Arkansas, on 2 December. By then, the Army of Missouri could muster just 6,000 troops. During the raid, Price's troopers had covered 1,424 miles, fought 43 engagements, and suffered 50 percent casualties. Although he had succeeded in diverting Federal resources from operations east of the Mississippi, Price's raid failed as a recruitment drive, and St. Louis remained fixed under Federal control.

Price's raid ended major combat operations in the Trans-Mississippi. The final fighting in the theater took place on 13 May 1865, at Palmito Ranch, near Brownsville, but by then General Robert E. Lee had surrendered his Army of Northern Virginia at Appomattox. After four years of fighting, the Civil War was over.

Analysis

Ever since the start of the war, weak leadership undermined the Confederacy's operations in the Trans-Mississippi. In 1861, disputes between Generals McCulloch and Price prevented coordination of military efforts, robbing the Confederates of an opportunity to seize Missouri and to compel the Federals to invest greater resources in securing the Trans-Mississippi. In 1862, Generals Van Dorn and Hindman had overestimated the capabilities of their men while proving themselves unequal to the contingencies of warfare. General Kirby Smith added a significant degree of professionalism to the department, but he lacked strategic judgment, hampering General Taylor, his most-skilled subordinate, and giving too much latitude to General Price, his least-skilled subordinate.

Although friction and poor generalship also bedeviled the Union, the overall organization and command structure in the Federal forces had given the United States a tremendous advantage in securing strategic objectives in the Trans-Mississippi. Since the outbreak of war, the United States had regarded the Mississippi River as the key terrain feature in the theater and had devoted the resources and personnel necessary to control it. The Union command structure facilitated cooperation between commanders on either side of the Mississippi and allowed the Federals to shift troops according to need.

From the outset, the Federals had identified Missouri as a vital strategic center in the Trans-Mississippi and had moved accordingly to secure it. General Curtis was the right man for the task; his victory at Pea Ridge in 1862 was arguably the most important event in the Trans-Mississippi. Had the Confederates succeeded at Pea Ridge, the doorway to St. Louis would have been open. A Confederate campaign to take the city, particularly at that stage of the war, would have required a substantial shift in Union resources away from theaters east of the river. Instead, Pea Ridge left the Confederates crippled and allowed Curtis to begin campaigning for control of Arkansas. While Prairie Grove was neither as large nor as dramatic as Pea Ridge, its strategic importance lay in sealing the doorway to Missouri. Harassment by Confederate guerrillas and Price's horsemen notwithstanding, Missouri and St. Louis would remain in Union hands.

Union performance in Louisiana was less spectacular. Banks lacked the military training and skills necessary to manage either a department or an army in the field. His missteps along the Bayou Teche and the Sabine River in 1863, and his blunders on the Red River in 1864, meant that the Federals failed to capture western Louisiana and Texas. Fortunately for the North, Kirby Smith passed up the opportunity to capture Banks' army and Porter's fleet at Alexandria. As Taylor reflected, "such opportunities never occur twice." Indeed, the capacity to take advantage of opportunities ultimately was the difference between success and failure in the Trans-Mississippi.

The Author

Jeffery S. Prushankin received his Ph.D. in United States history from the University of Arkansas in 2000 and was awarded a West Point summer fellowship in 2002. He taught American military history at Penn State Abington and currently is the professor of Civil War Era studies at Millersville University in Lancaster, Pennsylvania. His area of specialization is the war in the Trans-Mississippi South and he is the author of numerous articles and books on that subject, most notably, *A Crisis in Confederate Command: Edmund Kirby Smith, Richard Taylor, and the Army of the Trans-Mississippi.* He is currently writing a military biography of General Edmund Kirby Smith.

FURTHER READINGS

Johnson, Ludwell H. *Red River Campaign: Politics and Cotton in the Civil War.* Baltimore: Johns Hopkins University Press, 1958; reprint, Kent, Ohio: Kent State University Press, 1993.

Kerby, Robert L. *Kirby Smith's Confederacy: The Trans-Mississippi South, 1863–1865.* New York: Columbia University Press, 1972.

Piston, William Garrett and Richard W. Hatcher III. *Wilson's Creek: The Second Battle of the Civil War and the Men Who Fought It.* Chapel Hill: University of North Carolina Press, 2000.

Prushankin, Jeffery S. *A Crisis in Confederate Command: Edmund Kirby Smith, Richard Taylor, and the Army of the Trans-Mississippi.* Baton Rouge: Louisiana State University Press, 2005.

Shea, William L. *Fields of Blood: The Prairie Grove Campaign.* Chapel Hill: University of North Carolina Press, 2009.

Shea, William L. and Earl J. Hess. *Pea Ridge: Civil War Campaign in the West.* Chapel Hill: University of North Carolina Press, 1992.

For more information on the U.S. Army in the Civil War, please read other titles in the U.S. Army Campaigns of the Civil War series published by the U.S. Army Center of Military History (www.history.army.mil).

Printed in Great Britain
by Amazon